IT'S TIME TO EAT LEEK

It's Time to Eat
LEEK

Walter the Educator

Silent King Books
A WhichHead Entertainment Imprint

Copyright © 2025 by Walter the Educator

All rights reserved. No part of this book may be reproduced in any manner whatsoever without written per- mission except in the case of brief quotations embodied in critical articles and reviews.

First Printing, 2024

Disclaimer

This book is a literary work; the story is not about specific persons, locations, situations, and/or circumstances unless mentioned in a historical context. Any resemblance to real persons, locations, situations, and/or circumstances is coincidental. This book is for entertainment and informational purposes only. The author and publisher offer this information without warranties expressed or implied. No matter the grounds, neither the author nor the publisher will be accountable for any losses, injuries, or other damages caused by the reader's use of this book. The use of this book acknowledges an understanding and acceptance of this disclaimer.

It's Time to Eat LEEK is a collectible early learning book by Walter the Educator suitable for all ages belonging to Walter the Educator's Time to Eat Book Series. Collect more books at WaltertheEducator.com

USE THE EXTRA SPACE TO TAKE NOTES AND DOCUMENT YOUR MEMORIES

LEEK

It's time to eat, hooray, hooray!

It's Time to Eat

Leek

A tasty treat is on the way!

Long and green, so fresh and sweet,

A yummy leek is fun to eat!

Leeks grow tall and leeks grow bright,

With leaves so green and stalks so white.

Pull them up and wash them clean,

Chop them up, so crisp and lean!

In a soup or in a stew,

Leeks bring flavor bright and new!

Soft and tender, warm and light,

Every bite is just so right!

Sauté them slow, watch them sizzle,

Hear them pop and watch them drizzle!

Golden brown and smelling sweet,

Leeks can make your meal complete!

It's Time to Eat

Leek

Leeks with butter, leeks with rice,

Leeks with pasta, oh, so nice!

Eat them raw or cook them well,

Every way, they taste so swell!

If you like a little crunch,

Try a leek inside your lunch!

Wrap it up or slice it thin,

Take a bite and smile big!

Leeks are cousins of the onion,

But they don't make tears come runnin'!

Mild and mellow, soft and neat,

They're a veggie hard to beat!

Leeks can help to keep you strong,

Eat them up the whole day long!

It's Time to Eat

Leek

Full of goodness, full of cheer,

Try some leeks throughout the year!

Time to taste, let's take a bite,

Crunchy, munchy, pure delight!

Soft and silky, warm or cool,

Leeks are such a super fuel!

So grab a leek and take a chew,

Try it fresh or in a stew!

Eat it up and you will see,

It's Time to Eat

Leek

Leeks are yummy, just for me!

ABOUT THE CREATOR

Walter the Educator is one of the pseudonyms for Walter Anderson. Formally educated in Chemistry, Business, and Education, he is an educator, an author, a diverse entrepreneur, and he is the son of a disabled war veteran. "Walter the Educator" shares his time between educating and creating. He holds interests and owns several creative projects that entertain, enlighten, enhance, and educate, hoping to inspire and motivate you. Follow, find new works, and stay up to date with Walter the Educator™

at WaltertheEducator.com

www.ingramcontent.com/pod-product-compliance
Lightning Source LLC
LaVergne TN
LVHW052013060526
838201LV00059B/4004